WHY YOUR WORDS DON'T COME TO PASS

The Six Absolute Reasons You Have Not Seen A Manifestation of Your Words

FRANCIS JONAH

IMPORTANT

My name is Francis Jonah. I believe all things are possible. It is because of this belief that I have achieved so much in life. This belief extends to all. I believe every human being is equipped to succeed in every circumstance, regardless of the circumstance.

I know the only gap that exists between you and what you need to achieve or overcome is knowledge.

People are destroyed for lack of knowledge.

It is for this reason that I write short practical books that are so simple, people begin to experience immediate results as evidenced by the many testimonies I receive on a daily basis for my various books.

This book is no exception. You will obtain results because of it.

Visit my website for powerful articles and materials

www.francisjonah.com

FREE GIFTS

Just to say Thank You for downloading my book, I'd like to give you these books for free.

Download these 4 powerful books today for free and give yourself a great future.

Click Here to Download

Your testimonies will abound. Click Here to see my other books. They have produced many testimonies and I want your testimony to be one too.

Counselling Or Prayer

Send me an email if you need prayer or counsel or you have a question.

Better still if you want to make my acquaintance

My email is drfrancisjonah@gmail.com

Other books by Francis Jonah

3 Day Fasting Challenge: How to receive manifestation of answers

How to Have Outrageous Financial Abundance In No Time:Biblical Principles For Immediate And Overwhelming Financial Success

5 Bible Promises, Prayers and Decrees That Will Give You The Best Year Ever: A book for Shaping Every Year Successfully plus devotional (Book Of Promises 1)

Influencing The Unseen Realm: How to Influence The Spirit Realm for Victory in The Physical Realm(Spiritual Success Books)

Prayer That Works: Taking Responsibility For Answered Prayer

Healing The Sick In Five Minutes:How Anyone Can Heal Any Sickness

The Financial Miracle Prayer

The Best Secret To Answered Prayer

The Believer's Authority(Authority Of The Believer,Power And Authority Of The Believer)

The Healing Miracle Prayer

I Shall Not Die: Secrets To Long Life And Overcoming The Fear of Death

Three Straightforward Steps To Outrageous Financial Abundance: Personal Finance (Finance Made Easy Book 1)

Prayers For Financial Miracles: And 3 Ways To Receive Answers Quickly

Book: 3 Point Blueprint For Building Strong Faith: Spiritual:Religious:Christian:Motivational

How To Stop Sinning Effortlessly

The Power Of Faith-Filled Words

All Sin Is Paid For: An Eye Opening Book

Be Happy Now:No More Depression

The Ultimate Christian: How To Win In Every Life Situation: A book full of Revelations

Books:How To Be Free From Sicknesses And Diseases(Divine Health): Divine Health Scriptures

Multiply Your Personal Income In Less Than 30 Days

Ultimate Method To Memorize The Bible Quickly: (How To Learn Scripture Memorization)

Overcoming Emotional Abuse

Passing Exams The Easy Way: 90% and above in exams (Learning Simplified)

Books:Goal Setting For Those In A Hurry To Achieve Fast

Do Something Lest You Do Nothing

Financial Freedom:My Personal Blue-Print Made Easy For Men And Women

Why Men Go To Hell

Budgeting Tools And How My Budget Makes Me More Money

How To Raise Capital In 72 Hours: Quickly and Effectively Raise Capital Easily in Unconventional Ways (Finance Made Easy)

How To Love Unconditionally

Financial Independence: The Simple Path I Used To Wealth

Finding Happiness: The Story Of John Miller: A Christian Fiction

Finance Made Easy (2 Book Series)

Click here to see my author page

Contents

INTRODUCTION

CHAPTER ONE

CHAPTER TWO

CHAPTER THREE

CHAPTER FOUR

CHAPTER FIVE

CHAPTER SIX

INTRODUCTION

Words carry power and are the creative force of the universe. This very earth with everything in it whether visible or invisible was created by words. God spoke them into being.

This much the scriptures make clear:

By faith we understand that the worlds were framed by the word of God, so that the things which are seen were not made of things which are visible.

Hebrews 11:2

Words can bring life and at the same time bring death. Words can heal as well as break. Words can set your life in a positive or negative direction.

The book of proverbs takes time to tell us about the power of words:

A man's stomach shall be satisfied from the fruit of his mouth; from the produce of his lips he shall be filled. 21 Death and life are in the power of the tongue, and those who love it will eat its fruit.

Proverbs 18:20–21

The fruit of your mouth and the produce of your lips signify the results of the words you speak. This means your words can determine your results in life.

The scriptures are filled with so many men of faith who did amazing things through the power of their words. Our Lord Jesus Christ who is our best example taught us in deed and in word, how we can achieve extraordinary and amazing things through words.

He spoke to the storm of the sea and it obeyed. He commanded blind eyes and they opened. He provided food for more than five thousand people by his words.

He spoke to a fish to provide him with money and it obeyed. He spoke to a fig tree to die and it died. He spoke to the dead to come back to life and it happened according to his words.

Apart from proving to us the power of words, Jesus clearly told us our words can also come to pass and produce great results.

This remains one of the most amazing scriptures in the Bible:

So Jesus answered and said to them, have faith in God. 23 For assuredly, I say to you, whoever says to this mountain, 'Be removed and be cast into the sea,' and does not doubt in his heart, but believes that those things he says will be done, he will have whatever he says.

Mark 11:22–23

This is so beautiful. Jesus tells us that we will have what we say. Although words are powerful and produce significant results, there are so many people whose words never come to pass. This is because they miss one or more of the several key principles that cause the manifestation of words.

The fact that what you are saying is in line with the written word of God does not mean it will necessarily come to pass. The point is that beyond what you are saying, it takes the coming together of other things for your words to manifest.

These key principles revealed by God in His word for your words come to pass will be revealed to you soon.

People who lack the understanding of these fundamental keys go about speaking words which never come to pass. Some of them wonder why their words failed to manifest and conclude that this teaching is not true.

Some even claim that if it is true, it may be for certain special or anointed people. Irrespective of what you may have experienced or what someone told you, I want you to understand that the truth still stands that words are powerful and have influence on every single person on the face of this earth.

There are many who have quoted scriptures to disprove the power of words and have found strange explanations for why you must not apply the power of words. This is because many people have been disappointed due to the results they got when they tried to walk in the revelation of the power of words.

Our experiences can never disprove the word of God. The Bible is clear that God should be true and every other man a liar:

Rom 3:4 God forbid: yea, let God be true, but every man a liar; as it is written, That thou mightest be justified in thy sayings, and mightest overcome when thou art judged.

Romans 3:4

God doesn't lie, His words are infallible. It is man that lies and we cannot take man's word over God's word:

Num 23:19 God is not a man, that he should lie; neither the son of man, that he should repent: hath he said, and shall he not do it? or hath he spoken, and shall he not make it good?

Numbers 23:19

The key principles you would need to know are given in this book and I am confident that if you meditate and give these principles time and do them without forgetting them, you will come back with a testimony.

Beloved, many people speak the word of God but end up not seeing it come to pass in their lives. This has left many of them frustrated.

Some have even questioned the integrity of God's word. This is really a clear-cut situation, man cannot have more integrity than God. God Himself has exalted His word above His name. That goes to show the integrity of the word of God.

Psa 138:2 I will worship toward thy holy temple, and praise thy name for thy lovingkindness and for thy truth: for thou hast magnified thy word above all thy name.

Psalm 138:2

Personally, I strongly believe everything Jesus said about the power of the word of God in our mouths.

This is the secret that took my life from sickness into good health, lack into abundance and from struggling into unending success.

In the presence of several people my words have caused shorter legs to grow, healed the sick, and brought abundance to the poor and hope to the hopeless.

I have had other experiences where my words have not manifested, it didn't make me right and the word of God wrong. God's word is supreme.

Indeed, the power of words is unlimited and infinite. The fact that you spoke and it never came to pass does not mean there is something wrong with the word of God. When you have such an attitude, you will never make progress.

Know that the problem is from you and then you can find the problem and rectify it.

There are reasons your words have failed to materialize and I will gladly show you these reasons and how to deal with them.

I will outline seven reasons revealed from the Word of God that explains why the words of many of

God's children don't come to pass. I will offer scriptural and Word based solutions to every single hindrance to the manifestation of your words at the end of each chapter. This will help you deal with each specific hindrance.

The revelations I offer in this book have helped countless people and it will surely do the same thing in your life. I guarantee you a deeper understanding that will usher you into realm where your words will begin to produce results.

Let us delve into the reasons why your words do not come to pass.

CHAPTER ONE

WORDS NOT FOUNDED ON PERSONAL REVELATION

In this chapter, I am going to show you the first reason why the words of some believers don't come to pass.

It is important to know that what gives the power of manifestation to your words is the foundation on which it stands.

Whether your words will come to pass or not depends on whether it is founded on the opinion of men or the everlasting and living word of God.

Personal Revelation, Not Just Written Words

For your words to come to pass, you must speak words that are founded on the revelation of God's word.

No matter how loud or forceful you are in your words, until it is founded on a personal revelation of the word of God, it will be difficult to see any significant manifestations.

Moreover, going around quoting scriptures does not automatically guarantee that those scriptures will come to pass. The truth is that, the devil and his cohorts can also quote scriptures. Their quoting doesn't make those scriptures come to pass.

More often than not, quotations are not spoken from a place of understanding and conviction.

I have seen so many Christians who go about quoting scriptures such as "by his stripes I am healed, I am rich and prosperous because Jesus became poor that I might become rich, I am the righteousness of God in Christ" and so many fine scriptures that tell us who we are and what we have in Christ.

After quoting all these scriptures many of them see nothing.

You see, if the Bible says by his stripes you are healed, it is trying to communicate something to you. Many do not get what is being communicated and just quote the scripture. This is why personal revelation is important. You need to understand the revelation behind the scripture.

It is true that quoting the scriptures can bring you to the place of understanding and illumination so that you can now speak the words that will ensure your total healing. The key is to get to that place of understanding and illumination.

Those who speak based on their personal revelation of this scripture begin to understand that if by his stripes they are healed, then sickness cannot continue to prevail in their body.

Therefore, instead of by his stripes I am healed alone, they speak to the ailment to get out of their bodies. They have realized they are healed and cannot be entertaining the sickness so they speak the right words. Sickness out of my body, I cannot entertain you if I am already healed.

At this juncture, you will realize that they are speaking from personal revelation founded on the word of God and not just quoting scripture.

The secret most people miss here is that it is not just the written word of God that one puts into his mouth and speaks that will come to pass but rather speaking words that are founded on your personal revelation that you received from the scriptures concerning a particular situation. You must fully understand what you are saying. It must illuminate your spirit.

Let us look at two examples that will clarify the difference between quoting scriptures and speaking based on personal revelation.

Jesus' encounter with the devil in his temptation is a clear example of how quoting what is written may not even move the devil.

Let us look at the account here:

Then Jesus was led up by the Spirit into the wilderness to be tempted by the devil. 2 And when He had fasted forty days and forty nights, afterward He was hungry. 3 Now when the tempter came to Him, he said, if you are the Son of God, command that these stones become bread. 4 But He answered and said, it is written, Man shall not live by bread alone, but by every word that proceeds from the mouth of God. Then the devil took Him up into the holy city, set Him on the pinnacle of the temple, 6 and said to Him, if you are the Son of God, throw yourself down. For it is written: He shall give His angels charge over you, and, in their hands they shall bear you up, lest you dash your foot against a stone. 7 Jesus said to him, it is written again, you shall not tempt the LORD your God. Again, the devil took Him up on an exceedingly high mountain, and showed Him all the kingdoms of the world and their glory. 9 And he said to Him, all these things I will give you if you will fall down and worship me. 10 Then Jesus said to him, away with you, Satan! For it is written, you shall worship the LORD your God, and Him only you shall serve. 11 Then the devil left Him, and behold, angels came and ministered to Him.

Matthew 4:1-11.

You will notice in the above scripture that as long as Jesus quoted what was written in the scriptures the devil persisted in his manoeuvres.

The point is this, quoting what is written does not have the same power of influence as speaking or making a command based on the revelation of the word.

Quoting what is written will not move the devil away. Quoting what is written will not guarantee manifestation of your words. It can be taken as a mere giving of information. This is critical.

When Jesus kept on saying "it is written", there was no power in it to cause a manifestation of his heart desires. His desires were simple, that the devil would leave him alone.

What is written in the Bible is the letter of the word. The letter of the word lacks the power and efficacy to influence and enforce the kind of change one desires. The Bible clearly distinguishes them:

Who also made us sufficient as ministers of the new covenant, not of the letter but of the Spirit; for the letter kills, but the spirit gives life.

2 Corinthians 3:6

The letter or just the written words kill. They do not produce any results on their own. However, if the Holy Spirit quickens and opens your eyes to what is written, that very truth becomes the foundation of the kind of words that have the capacity to manifest when spoken.

Those very words cease to be the written word but words that are inspired and filled with God's breadth and power specifically given to you for a specific need within a specific time frame.

Revelation is when the power of the Holy Spirit comes on the written word, quickens it and opens your eyes to see that word as a personal word from God to deal with a specific need in your life. At this moment, this word ceases to be a written word but words that contain power ready to come to pass when spoken.

The revelation word is normally what is deduced from the written word by the power of the Holy Spirit.

For His word was with authority and ability and weight and power.

Luke 4:32. Amplified

When Jesus recognized that just speaking what is written will not amount to much but rather a revealed truth that one has received from God, he no longer responded to the devil on the basis of what was just written. Instead, he spoke based on the very word he received from the Holy Spirit at that moment.

He knew to put the devil to flight with his words and not just quote scripture. Scripture had its place in helping Jesus not to succumb to the devils temptations.

For the devil to go away, Jesus used different kind of words. Watch the scriptures carefdully:

Again, the devil took Him up on an exceedingly high mountain, and showed Him all the kingdoms of the world and their glory. 9 And he said to Him, all these things I will give you if you will fall down and worship me. 10 THEN JESUS SAID TO HIM, AWAY WITH YOU, SATAN! Then the devil left Him, and behold, angels came and ministered to Him.

Matthew 4:8-10.

Jesus could have said it is written "You shall serve no other God besides me", which is actually true and accurately written in the scriptures but that was not going to drive the devil away.

How many devils and diseases are still hovering around your life because you are quoting scripture instead of speaking words based on revelation.

If you really noticed the scriptures we read, the devil was also quoting scriptures.

Then the devil took Him up into the holy city, set Him on the pinnacle of the temple, 6 and said to Him, if you are the Son of God, throw yourself down. For it is written: He shall give His angels charge over you, and, in their hands they shall bear you up, lest you dash your foot against a stone.

You can clearly see the devil quoting the written word comfortably.

What made the devil leave him was when he addressed him specifically by saying "away with you" and immediately that word came to pass.

The devil fled from him immediately. This explains why the words of many people have failed to come to pass even though they were consistently speaking what is written in the scriptures.

What is written is written but will not just come to pass because it is spoken. On the other hand if what is written is the foundation by which we receive revelation in order to deal with our present needs and speak the right words, we will receive manifestation.

The principle to pick from here is that it is words from personal revelations that have the power to come to pass when spoken.

Always remember that every word you speak or action you initiate which is not founded on the revealed truth of God's word will hardly come to pass.

Turn the Written Word to Revelation Word

To bring yourself to a place where your words will always come to pass, be acquainted with the word of God through persistent meditation and prayer and the moment the Holy Spirit quickens the word, He will tell you what you must say and surely your words will eventually come to pass.

Don't just go around quoting scriptures in the name of speaking words but speak words based on the revelation from the written word.

In case you find yourself in any challenge, make time to meditate on scriptures that talk about your challenge.

As you prayerfully meditate on the written word, the Holy Spirit will give you words you must speak and as you speak them out, surely they will come to pass.

Concluding example

When you read a scripture like this:

Mat 8:17 That it might be fulfilled which was spoken by Esaias the prophet, saying, Himself took our infirmities, and bare our sicknesses.

Matthew 8:17

You must not go around just quoting this scripture; you must get the revelation behind it and speak that revelation.

What is the revelation behind this scripture? It is to tell you that you cannot be carrying sicknesses that Jesus has already carried.

Glory to God.

Thus, you do not necessarily quote the scripture, what you do is to speak to the devil and the sickness to leave your body because Jesus has already carried it.

This kind of speaking is what will bring the results you are looking for. When you just quote the scripture, you are doing what the devil can also do. Go deeper, get the revelation behind the word and you will know what to do and say.

In the next chapter, I will show you the second reason why the words of some people do not come to pass and how to deal with it.

CHAPTER TWO

UNBELIEF

The next reason why the words of many do not come to bass is unbelief.

Maybe you needed healing in your body, or you are facing a financial challenge and have spoken the word of God that "by his stripes you were healed" or declared that "you are rich" and yet those words have not come to pass.

It is likely that your words are hindered from manifesting because of unbelief.

You may be wondering—why hasn't my words come to pass even though I spoke what is in line with a revelation from God's word?

Whenever you are confronted with such a situation, it could be a matter of speaking the word of God in unbelief. Jesus said that right in the gospel of Matthew.

So Jesus said to them, because of your unbelief; for assuredly, I say to you, if you have faith as a mustard seed, you will say to this mountain, 'Move from here to there,' and it will move; and nothing will be impossible for you. Matthew 17:20, KJV

The point is that, it is unbelief, not the will of God that is the cause of so much defeat in the lives of believers as far as manifestation of their words is concerned.

Unbelief is key in shooting down every faith filled words spoken by God's children. It is one of the weapons that works against the saints.

It's not that we don't want to believe, for the most part; it's that we haven't learned how to overcome the tiniest bit of unbelief that resides in our hearts.

That slight lack of confidence in what we are speaking. That is what unbelief is.

Often, we don't even know it's there until we take a closer look.

When we come to God, our confidence must be absolute.

There is the unbelief which is a total hardening of heart towards what you said. It can also be that you do not belpower at all. This is not the problem of most believers. They actually believe what they are saying yet, more often than not, their confidence is not absolute.

A heart of unbelief grieves God. Hence you can be speaking faith filled words and still be in unbelief. Just as unbelief can hinder you from receiving from God, it can also hinder your words from coming to pass irrespective of whether that word is a personal revelation from God.

This is the problem with several believers, even though they are speaking what God told them, they are still not absolutely sure in their mind that it will come to pass. This unbelief in their heart is what explains why their words never come to pass.

Why is belief so important to deal with? Because, ***"If you can believe, <u>ALL</u> things are possible" (Mark 9:23, NKJV).***

That means you can call the dead back to life and it will happen. You can command money and in no time, it will appear. You can command the paralyzed to walk and it will come to pass.

That's where God wants us to live—in the realm of what is possible through Him, and Him alone and the word of God in our mouth. This is what sets believers apart from a lost and dying world.

Therefore, the second reason why you don't see the full manifestation of your words is that you don't believe your words completely. If you believe your words completely, they will surely come to pass when you speak them. That was exactly what

Jesus revealed to his disciples about the fulfilling power of spoken words:

For assuredly, I say to you, whoever says to this mountain, 'Be removed and be cast into the sea,' and does not doubt in his heart, but believes that those things he says will be done, he will have whatever he says. Mark 11:23–24

In the above scripture Jesus is showing us two important principles that will surely cause every word you speak come to pass.

That means you can tell sickness to leave and it will be so. You can command money into your account and it will happen.

You can command the rain to fall in your city and it will obey you just as Joshua spoke to the moon and the sun and they stood for more than a day:

Then Joshua spoke to the LORD in the day when the LORD delivered up the Amorites before the children of Israel, and he said in the sight of Israel: Sun, stand still over Gibeon; and Moon, in the Valley of Aijalon. 13 So the sun stood still, and the moon stopped, till the people had revenge upon their enemies. Joshua 10:12–13).

The condition here is that whatever you speak, you must believe absolutely. He said you must believe that those words you spoke will come to pass. This is where so many Christians are defeated. Let me give you an example to explain what I mean by this.

I Stopped The Rain From Falling

Sometime ago I was out to shop at the market with one of my spiritual sons. The moment we set out the weather started changing and the clouds were heavily forming. That means the rains was going to be pouring down any moment from then. The best thing to do at that time was for us to return back home for the rain to stop before we can return back to the market.

Instantly I felt that I could exercise my authority. I looked at the clouds in the presence of my son and declared that this rain is not coming now until we return back home. I said to my son, I have put the rain on hold and until we are fully done and return home this rain is no going to fall.

At that time my son became uneasy but he had to follow me anyway. When we were almost about entering the market the clouds became thicker and darker. Everything showed that the rain was coming in few minutes. Immediately my son said to me, sir the rain is coming.

I responded son, what I have said is final therefore ignore all the signs because until we get home no rain is coming. We went on and purchased everything that we needed and to the glory of God, the clouds that had fully formed and was supposed to fall cleared off. We finished everything and return back home.

Later on in the evening, the rains came back. The problem with many people is that their belief is so strong and voracious at the time they spoke the word but the moment that word is tested and everything appears that the word they spoke will never materialize they begin to lose their belief. The moment certain things appear contrary to the word they spoke they immediately believe what they are seeing as against what they spoke.

They Don't Believe their Words to The End

I have met several people who had the privilege of listening to messages or read books about the power of words.

When they are confronted with any form of challenge or need, they immediately put their faith to work and begin to speak faith-filled words. If they are facing a health problem, they declare that by his stripes they are healed.

If they have a financial need, they call for money to come. If they are confronted with any storm of life they speak and declare peace and calmness. When obstacles try to stop them from making progress they declare that the obstacle is completely removed.

Nonetheless, immediately things begin to turn contrary to their words they begin to lose their ground and give in to that situation. In the midst of their faith-filled words, the moment their health begins to get worse they begin to waver in their belief.

Their belief shifts from their words and the foundation of the word of God to how bad things are getting and eventually causes a complete death of what they spoke in the past. This is a clear sign that their confidence was not absolute in what they said.

Full confidence you are a man

If I ask you if you are a man, you will have 100% confidence in your answer.

However if I ask you the colour of your intestines, some may give me an answer which may be correct but their confidence will not be as the answer for their gender.

That is unbelief in action.

Like the people we were talking about, they commanded the door to open, the money to come or that opportunity to show up in their life but when things start turning contrary to their words they give up and those words never comes to pass. Many at time, the only consolation they rely on is that may be it is not the will of God for them to enjoy whatever they desired for.

The will of God is very important but many a time, what they speak is the will of God. Things like healing, prosperity and increase are the will of God.

The point is very clear, the fact that you believe at the start when you speak words does not mean those words will just manifest.

Jesus is showing you that the price to cause the manifestation of every word you speak is to believe from the start until the words manifest irrespective of what comes to fight against your words.

I would have lost my words if I had believed the clouds that came to show that my words are null and void. What caused the manifestation of my words was my solid belief even in the midst of concrete evidence that what I said was not going to happen.

Jesus Persisted Until the Fig Tree Died

According to Mark 11, Jesus spoke to a fig tree that it will never bear fruit again. Even though these words were heard by his disciples who were with him, the bible records that nothing happened. This really made the disciples surprised.

The account is as follows:

Now the next day, when they had come out from Bethany, He was hungry. 13 And seeing from afar a fig tree having leaves, He went to see if perhaps He would find something on it. When He came to it, He found nothing but leaves, for it was not the season for figs. 14 In response Jesus said to it, let no one eat fruit from you ever again. And His disciples heard it. Mk 11:12–14

Jesus himself was fully aware that whatever a person speaks is real but takes time to manifest in the physical world. He also knew that every word that is spoken will be tested and that with the power of absolute believe those words will surely manifest irrespective of the attack the enemy brings against it.

With this understanding, he did not bother to check if what he spoke was going to manifest or not. He needed not to be concerned about how fresh the tree looked like after his words were released.

It was not a surprise to him at all when the tree started dying from the root the very next day. The disciples were surprised because they never had this understanding. They were only moved by what they saw. Their belief was only attached to what they could see and feel. This is how many Christians are today. When they speak, they are excited it will come to pass but the moment things begin to go contrary to their words they believe that report and ignore what they said eventually losing out on what God wanted to do in their life.

How do we deal with this problem once and for all?

Believe During and After You Speak

The answer in what Jesus told Thomas in the book of John.

Jesus said to him, Thomas, because you have seen me, you have believed. Blessed are those who have not seen and yet have believed. John 20:29

If you will train yourself to believe your words during and after your words are spoken, all your words will eventually come into fruition.

Don't only believe when you speak those words at the beginning. Believe even if everything comes to show that what you said is false and impossible to manifest. It is only those who believe to the end that will see result. That is absolute confidence.

Blessed is she who believed, for there will be a fulfillment of those things which were told her from the Lord.

Luke 1:45

In the midst of real evidence which is contrary to your words, do what God did when he called those things which be not as though they are.

In the presence of Him whom he believed—God, who gives life to the dead and calls those things which do not exist as though they did.

Romans 4:17

When the doctor tells you the fact that you will not survive this condition, continue to maintain your ground of what you said which is consistent with the revelation of God's word.

The life of Abraham is a perfect example of what God wants you to do in order to bring to pass your spoken words.

The book of Roman 4:17-20 tells us that in the midst of tangible evidence which proved that it was too late for Abraham to give birth, he still believed his words.

The word God gave to him as the father of many nations became the words of his mouth. He spoke it until everyone got to know that he was the father of many nations. Even when some were laughing at him, he still believed in those words. When his wife Sarah had passed the age of child bearing, he maintained his belief in his words.

The scriptures put it beautifully:

(As it is written, I have made you a father of many nations) in the presence of Him whom he believed— God, who gives life to the dead and calls those things which do not exist as though they did; 18 who, contrary to hope, in hope believed, so that he became the father of many nations, according to what was spoken, So shall your descendants be. 19 And not being weak in faith, he did not consider his own body, already dead (since he was about a hundred years old),

and the deadness of Sarah's womb. 20 He did not waver at the promise of God through unbelief, but was strengthened in faith, giving glory to God, 21 and being fully convinced that what He had promised He was also able to perform. Romans 4:17–21

As far as Abraham was concerned, this was not just a written word but God's revelation to him, no wonder he persisted in his belief until it manifested. To us it was a written word meant to give us hope.

For whatever things were written before were written for our learning, that we through the patience and comfort of the Scriptures might have hope. Romans 15:4

To Abraham, this word was a revelation from God to him, meant to be spoken and believed even in the midst of all impossibilities.

But what does it say? The word is near you, in your mouth and in your heart (that is, the word of faith which we preach.

Romans 10:8

When Abraham fully maintained his belief in his words it eventually manifested at the end. Now that you have come to a recognition of one of the basic reasons why the words of so many people do not come to pass and have learnt how to deal with that hindrance, let us quickly move to the next chapter and discover the third reason your words do not come to pass.

CHAPTER THREE

DOUBT

The next reason your words do not come to pass is doubt. Jesus revealed this in his teaching in Mark 11:23:

> *Have faith in God. 23 For assuredly, I say to you, whoever says to this mountain, 'Be removed and be cast into the sea,' and does not doubt in his heart, but believes that those things he says will be done, he will have whatever he says.*
>
> *Mark 11:22–23*

Jesus is saying that another reason why your words are not coming to pass no matter how loudly and boldly they are spoken is doubt.

I have noticed that this is very common with so many people. They still live in doubt even when they declare God's word concerning their life.

The word of God clearly affirms that one of the greatest hindrances to the life of faith and the supernatural is doubt. Notice how James 1:6 reveals this:

But let him ask in faith, with no doubting, for he who doubts is like a wave of the sea driven and tossed by the wind. 7 For let not that man suppose that he will receive anything from the Lord; 8 he is a double-minded man, unstable in all his ways. James 1:6–8.

Not only does doubt carry the capacity to stop the manifestation of your prayers, but also the manifestation of every word that you speak.

What is doubt and how does it affect your words from coming to pass? Doubt is not an outright denial or unbelief(lack of absolute confidence), but an attitude or feeling of uncertainty. A wavering between one belief to another.

It mainly has to do with reconsidering what you believe. You first believe the thing will work, then you believe it will not work. This moving from one opinion to the other is what we call doubt.

Doubt is when one finds himself between two opinions. In the context of this book doubt is to waver between whether your words will come to pass or the circumstances you are seeing will overpower your words.

A person who doubts begins to withdraw the moment he sees contrary situations. The sad situation is that doubt will never get your words to manifest. The Bible is clear on it:

For let not that man suppose that he will receive anything from the Lord.

James 1:6

The moment a person doubts, he immediately loses whatever he possessed by faith. This is what happened to Peter. When he began to doubt because of the boisterous wind, he began to sink:

And Peter answered Him and said, Lord, if it is you, command me to come to You on the water.

29 So He said, "Come." And when Peter had come down out of the boat, he walked on the water to go to Jesus. 30 But when he saw that the wind was boisterous, he was afraid; and beginning to sink he cried out, saying, Lord, save me! 31 And immediately Jesus stretched out His hand and caught him, and said to him, O you of little faith, why did you doubt?

Matthew 14:28–31

Similarly, when you begin to doubt because you saw a contrary situation, you immediately lose out and those words you spoke immediately get shot down.

A doubting person is an unstable or divided man who lacks sufficient faith to lay hold of the promises of God given to him.

If you must know, doubt is a serious sin because it questions the integrity, goodness, character and faithfulness of God and His word. Unlike God who does not change, the doubting person is *"like a wave of the sea, blown and tossed by the wind",* such an individual should not think he will receive the manifestation of his spoken words.

If you cannot stick to one opinion or truth, it will be very difficult to receive from God.

Doubt is a thief and has robbed many of their blessing. Do not let it continue to rob you.

It is time to cure it permanently.

The Cure to Doubt

How can we deal with doubt so that every spoken word of God from our mouth will put on flesh? According to Jesus when you have little faith, doubt gains more strength in your heart.

31 And immediately Jesus stretched out His hand and caught him, and said to him, O you of little faith, why did you doubt? Matthew 14:31

If that is the case, how can we completely root out doubt in our heart?

The first thing to note is that doubt basically results from littleness of faith. When you have little faith in the spoken word of God, you will surely doubt when the waves begins to move. The moment you see certain contrary signs against your spoken words, you will begin to change your mind.

If you could develop absolute faith in your own words, there would be no room for doubt. It was faith in the words of men that gave you a job. Even though you never knew how much was in their account you took their words seriously and started working there.

Just as you will disregard any contrary information that anyone will bring to you, God also wants you to build strong faith in your words. When that happens no matter what happens, you know your words will surely come to pass.

In simple terms, whatever you say, consider it done. When you consider it done, you will not think if it will be done or not.

I am healed. I consider it done. There is no room to ask if I would be healed because I already consider it done.

Sometime ago, I was facing a challenge in my health. I waited on the Lord in prayer concerning that condition. In the course of the waiting, I had a vision in which a man appeared to me like a medical doctor and told me **"go it is done and you are healed"**.

Immediately I woke up I started declaring and speaking that I am healed. Even though the symptoms persisted, I was so sure that the Lord spoke to me so I could never have room for doubt.

Even in the midst of contrary thoughts, I still maintained my faith in what I heard the Lord told me in the dream.

In less than three days, all symptoms disappeared. My words came to pass because I had strong faith in the word I received from God in the dream. Understand that this word was founded on scripture and so I knew it was available for me.

Strong faith that displaces any kind of doubt is built on hearing from God and knowing that God spoke to you.

I was so sure I was healed that when I said it, doubt could not come near me. To deal with doubt consider your words done. Consider the revelation you had from God done.

When you hear from God, it is no longer mental assent but faith and when there is faith in your heart there would be no room for doubt concerning your words.

Let us quickly move to the next chapter and address the next thing that hinders the manifestation of spoken words.

CHAPTER FOUR

INCONSISTENCY IN YOUR WORDS

When you are inconsistent in your words, there is no way your words will come to pass. In this chapter, I am going to show why your words will not come to pass if you are inconsistent in your words and how to get rid of this hindrance.

It is important to note that anytime you engage in speaking any word given to you by God concerning any situation, the enemy will come at that very word.

Jesus in his teaching about the parable of the sower revealed to us that the enemy is fully aware of the power of spoken words and because of that will do everything possible to get rid of that word.

The sower sows the word. 15 And these are the ones by the wayside where the word is sown. When they hear, Satan comes immediately and takes away the word that was sown in their hearts.

Mark 4:14–15

The revelation here is that, Satan has a character of coming after every word of God you receive into your heart to be spoken.

Because he is fully aware of the capabilities of every word that proceeds from God, he will do everything possible to make sure that every spoken word must be shot down.

He does that by throwing all kinds of tests the moment a word is released from a child of God. The moment you declare that by his stripes you were healed, he will come at that word with a test.

The moment you call for that money to come, he will begin to stir situations that will make it look like the money will never come.

Immediately you spoke that word, circumstances that are contrary will begin to show up. This is where so many people who do not know the operations of the devil respond wrongly by speaking contrary words.

Instantly they start speaking and talking about the very contrary situation instead of maintaining their solid ground of consistently speaking what God told them. Jesus gave a perfect definition of this group of people in Mark 4:16-17

"These likewise are the ones sown on stony ground who, when they hear the word, immediately receive it with gladness; 17 and they have no root in themselves, and so endure only for a time. Afterward, when tribulation or persecution arises for the word's sake, immediately they stumble. Mk 4:16–17

At the beginning they spoke the word with boldness and faith but the moment trials started showing up their confession changed. This is why their words never materialized.

The point is that, the materialization of your words depend largely on the words you spoke at the time of the test and not just what you spoke at the beginning. You must not negate your words with your own words.

They will cancel each other out.

The consistency of speaking what he told you matters a lot because that is what will make the devil to recognize that what you spoke is more real than what he might be bringing against you.

Even when everything is going against your words, God expect you to still say that "by his stripes I am healed" even if the doctor says it is too late or your body is telling you that you cannot make it.

When your customers are not responding to you maintain what you said in the morning that today will be the best sales of the week. Satan will bring so many evidences to press you to change your words. This is the stage that determines the strong in faith and the weak in faith. I have seen so many people who give up at this stage and eventually lose the words they spoke.

This must not be you. Maintain your confession in the midst of the tests. That is how you pass the test. Yes, it is a test and you must pass it for your words to manifest.

Be Consistent in your Words in the Midst of Tests

We can learn so much from Jesus on how we can maintain our grounds and still speak God's word in the midst of all storms, tests and impossibilities.

Jesus demonstrated this in so many situations which are recorded in the gospels. One of such examples is recorded in the book of John in which he exhibited steadfastness of words when he had a report of Lazarus sickness:

When Jesus heard that, He said, this sickness is not unto death, but for the glory of God, that the Son of God may be glorified through it.

John 11:4

The fact that they had to send messengers to Jesus and asked for his presence concerning Lazarus health condition showed that it was a serious case, yet Jesus told them *"this sickness is not unto death"*. Jesus maintained his confession that death will not be the end result of Lazarus sickness.

Even when he finally knew that Lazarus was dead, he never gave in to the spirit of death through his words. He maintained his words that Lazarus was sleeping.

These things He said, and after that He said to them, our friend Lazarus sleeps, but I go that I may wake him up. 12 Then His disciples said, Lord, if he sleeps he will get well. 13 However, Jesus spoke of his death, but they thought that He was speaking about taking rest in sleep.

John 11:11-13

As far as Jesus was concerned, you win or lose through your words. He was aware that the words we speak and utter in the midst of storms, adversities, sicknesses and even death is our verdict or acceptance. Our words determine our stand and so he maintained his stand that Lazarus was not dead but was sleeping. He was just going to wake him up.

It took the ignorance of the disciples for Jesus to come to their level and explain to them that Lazarus was dead. Even that was not a confession, it was an explanation to the level of those who had no understanding.

Your words pass verdicts on you:

For by your words you will be justified and acquitted, and by your words you will be condemned and sentenced.

Matthew 12:37. Amplified

As far as your words are concerned you cannot eat your cake and have it back. This is the secret many people are yet to recognize. In the case of Jesus he refused to recognize death; he never accepted the death verdict which was clear evidence to all. His consistency in speaking the same thing that Lazarus was not dead but asleep was re-echoed even at the grave yard.

Then they took away the stone from the place where the dead man was lying. And Jesus lifted up His eyes and said, Father, I thank You that You have heard Me. 42 And I know that You always hear Me, but because of the people who are standing by I said this, that they may believe that You sent Me. 43 Now when He had said these things, He cried with a loud voice, "LAZARUS, COME FORTH!"

John 11:41–43

There is something significant you need to recognize in this scripture. When you understand this, it will revolutionize your mindset. In raising Lazarus from the dead, Jesus never said **"Lazarus rise out from the dead",** instead he said *"Lazarus come forth".*

My point is that the two are not the same. Whereas the former is a command for a dead person to come back to life, the latter is a call for someone who is just standing in another room to come around.

The lesson you need to learn here is simple, be steadfast and consistent in every word that you speak, irrespective of whatever happens.

Assuming you declared that by his stripes you were healed and everything goes to point that you are going to die, God expect you to maintain that confession because the very words you speak are what will determine whether your healing will manifest or not.

The moment you switch your words and start saying things like **"looking at how my condition is I don't think I'm going to survive"**, so will it be to you.

If you can get to a point where you are not moved by what you feel, see or hear but only by the word of faith in your lips, you will surely come back with a testimony.

David maintained his words of victory when every sign showed that Goliath was going to kill him. Recognize that anytime you speak a word that is motivated by the Spirit of God, the kingdom of darkness will unleash their attacks and machinery on your spoken word, but your consistency in speaking what God says is your greatest key for manifestation of your words.

The moment you lose out on this, you have lost out on your manifestation. Your words in the midst of storms, attacks, test, and challenging moments opens or closes the door of the supernatural and miraculous.

You see, your words are a start button. When you push the button, it sets things in motion—either good or bad. When we speak words, all of heaven is waiting to hear what we will say so that our words can be acted upon.

The devil has no rights to us except what we give him through our words.

That's why Jesus said, *"By your words you will be justified, and by your words you will be condemned" (Matthew 12:37, NKJV).*

Don't be one of those that say I am rich today and then I am poor tomorrow.

Your words give your life direction, as you keep changing them, your direction keeps changing and you will make no progress.

Just like bits give direction to horses and rudders to ships, your tongue and therefore your words give you direction:

Jas 3:3 Behold, we put bits in the horses' mouths, that they may obey us; and we turn about their whole body.

Jas 3:4 Behold also the ships, which though they be so great, and are driven of fierce winds, yet are they turned about with a very small helm, whithersoever the governor listeth.

Jas 3:5 Even so the tongue is a little member, and boasteth great things. Behold, how great a matter a little fire kindleth!

James 3:3-5

Know what you want and speak it consistently. Don't change it in the face of opposition.

In the next chapter, I am going to show you the next thing that opposes the manifestation of the words that you speak.

My desire is to see your progress and prosperity and freedom from negative people and circumstances. Because of that, please permit me to introduce two courses that I believe passionately will help you.

1. To cure prayerlessness, an inconsistent prayer life and the pain of not enjoying all that God has made available to you,, click [here](#) to learn more about my [3 Day Course](#) on "How to Overcome prayerlessness" that will solve the problem of prayerlessness in your life.

2. To overcome the pain of not having enough money to live where you want, eat what you want to eat and be a blessing to the multitudes around you, I have created a [7 Day Financial Abundance](#)

[Course](#) that will deliver financial abundance to you quickly.

Click [here](#) to learn more about that course.

CHAPTER FIVE

IMPROPER APPLICATION OF FAITH

Improper application of faith is another major reason why so many people do not end up seeing the manifestation of their words.

In this chapter, I am going to address the fifth reason so many people speak words that never materialize.

The word of God shows categorically that the kingdom in which we live functions by faith.

There is absolutely nothing that can be received in this kingdom outside faith. Faith is what makes everything possible in the kingdom of God.

For assuredly, I say to you, if you have faith as a mustard seed, you will say to this mountain, move from here to there,' and it will move; and nothing will be impossible for you. Matthew 17:20

It takes faith to be saved.

For by grace you have been saved through faith. Ephesians 2:8

As a matter of fact, none of us can please God or walk with him outside faith.

But without faith it is impossible to please Him, for he who comes to God must believe that He is, and that He is a rewarder of those who diligently seek Him. Hebrews 11:6

Therefore in the same way it takes faith for your words to become real. As a matter of fact faith itself is a language that calls those things which be not as though they were.

God who gives life to the dead and calls those things which do not exist as though they did. Romans 4:17

The word of God shows us in Hebrews that one of the basic reasons why God's spoken word to the children of Israel did not come to pass was because they did not mix the word with faith.

For indeed the gospel was preached to us as well as to them; but the word which they heard did not profit them, not being mixed with faith in those who heard it. Hebrews 4:2

Their failure to take personal responsibility by adding faith to the word that God spoke concerning them was what hindered the word of God from manifesting.

According to God's spoken word, they were ordained to live a great life and enjoy the best of the earth.

God told them he will give them cities they did not build and they will live in a land flowing with milk and honey.

But I have said to you, you shall inherit their land, and I will give it to you to possess, a land flowing with milk and honey. I am the LORD your God, who has separated you from the peoples. Leviticus 20:24

If they had added faith to these words and acted according to the tenets of faith, those words would have become a reality in their life.

According to the word of God, they could not take possession because of their lack of faith.

And to whom did he swear that they should not enter his rest, but to those who disobeyed [who had not listened to his words and refused to be compliant or be persuaded]? So we see that they were not able to enter [into his rest], because of their unwillingness to adhere to and trust in and rely on God [unbelief had shut them out].

Hebrews 3:18-19

Their lack of faith shut them out from enjoying and seeing what was spoken concerning them. Even though God was ready to take them into the supernatural realm, because of their lack of faith they were not ready to see those words come to pass.

The believer though has faith, so a lack of faith is not the problem. The problem is that we are not applying our faith properly. This scripture tell us that we have been given the measure of faith:

Rom 12:3 For I say, through the grace given unto me, to every man that is among you, not to think of himself more highly than he ought to think; but to think soberly, according as God hath dealt to every man the measure of faith.

Romans 12:3

If we do not apply our faith to the words we speak, we will see no results. This is the case with so many people today.

Many people become frustrated and disappointed when their words never come to pass not realizing that the fault is not from God but the improper application of their faith is causing those words not to manifest.

Believing and speaking constitute faith and many have that going for them. That is not all though, there are other laws of faith that must be applied properly and the absence of that proper application is what causes a lot of problems in many lives.

You will find the seven laws of faith in my book "Experience The Impossible". It will help you apply your faith properly.

I have heard so many people complain that they spoke to the situation to stop but it never came to pass.

Someone told me sometime ago that he once commanded healing for a sister who was sick and at the point of death but the person still died. He wondered why the person still died even after his words were spoken according to what God told him.

I told him that his problem was the issue of improper application of faith and he shouted and said that cannot be true. I told him that faith does not give up even at the point of death. He had given up, he had applied his faith improperly.

I asked him if he had read the story of the Shunammite woman who lost her only son to death and refused to recognized death but acted in absolute faith which eventually led to the boy coming back to life.

And the child grew. Now it happened one day that he went out to his father, to the reapers. 19 And he said to his father, my head, my head! So he said to a servant, carry him to his mother. 20 When he had taken him and brought him to his mother, he sat on her knees till noon, and then died. 21 And she went up and laid him on the bed of the man of God, shut the door upon him, and went out. 22 Then she called to her husband, and said, please send me one of the young men and one of the donkeys, that I may run to the man of God and come back. 2 Ki 4:18–22

I further asked him whether he was aware that the prophet Elisha had to engage in a series of prayers before the boy came back to life.

Even when the boy was as good as dead the prophet never gave up until what they desired came to pass.

He laid his staff on the child, he prayed, he laid on the child with his whole body, he went down the house to pray, he laid on the child again, before the child rose.

Does this not teach you that real faith never gives up until it has received what has been spoken?

When Elisha came into the house, there was the child, lying dead on his bed. 33 He went in therefore, shut the door behind the two of them, and prayed to the LORD. 34 And he went up and lay on the child, and put his mouth on his mouth, his eyes on his eyes, and his hands on his hands; and he stretched himself out on the child, and the flesh of the child became warm. 35 He returned and walked back and forth in the house, and again went up and stretched himself out on him; then the child sneezed seven times, and the child opened his eyes. 36 And he called Gehazi and said, call this Shunammite woman. So he called her. And when she came in to him, he said, "Pick up your son. 2 Ki 4:32–36

Faith does not give up until what is desired manifests.

Listen carefully.

People give up after one hour; some give up after a day, others after a week.

Those who operate faith properly do not give up until they get the answer. Write it down. Let it stick in your heart and mind.

That is how Elijah prayed for rain:

1Ki 18:42 So Ahab went up to eat and to drink. And Elijah went up to the top of Carmel; and he

cast himself down upon the earth, and put his face between his knees,

1Ki 18:43 And said to his servant, Go up now, look toward the sea. And he went up, and looked, and said, There is nothing. And he said, Go again seven times.

1Ki 18:44 And it came to pass at the seventh time, that he said, Behold, there ariseth a little cloud out of the sea, like a man's hand. And he said, Go up, say unto Ahab, Prepare thy chariot, and get thee down, that the rain stop thee not.

1 Kings 18:42-44

Faith does not give in irrespective of what comes against the spoken word but endures until the words come to pass.

Therefore, the fact that he declared some words of healing over a sick person does not mean death will not come knocking but what he was expected to do was to still maintain his faith and not give in to death which would have brought the person back to life.

He finally became convinced that he missed this aspect of the faith teaching at that time. He told me, Sir if I knew this revelation by then, the lady would have been alive by now.

I have a similar story. I commanded a young man whose left leg was short for it to become the same. After several minutes nothing happened.

Those in the convention were anxious. A few leaders wanted to deliver me from the embarrassment.

A few people began to cry. I just persisted and kept speaking to the leg. All of a sudden, 15 minutes later, I heard screams. An usher had seen the leg become the same.

The young man suddenly jumped up to celebrate the victory he had gained.

I was not only relieved, I learned a powerful lesson on persistence. Faith always works when applied properly.

If you do not properly mix your spoken words with real enduring faith don't expect them to come to pass.

Let me quickly highlight what faith truly is and show you how you can properly mix your faith with words so that your words will always come to pass.

What is Faith?

The book of Hebrews 11:1 gives us a perfect definition of faith.

Now faith is the assurance (the confirmation, title deed) of the things [we] hope for, being the proof of things [we] do not see and the conviction of their reality [faith perceiving as real fact what is not revealed to the senses]. Hebrews 11:1. Amplified

Did you notice the words used in the definition of faith? **"Assurance"**, **"confirmation"**, **"title deed"**, **"proof"**, and **"conviction of reality"**. These are strong words. That means if you have assurance that the words you spoke will come to pass, absolutely nothing can stop it from manifesting.

If you have the confirmation that your healing will manifest according to your words, there would be no room for doubt. Have you ever had a confirmation on your phone message inbox about some amount of money sent to you and still doubted that the money is in your account?

That cannot be possible. Another strong word that defines faith is **"title deed"**. A **"title deed"** is a legal document constituting evidence of right of ownership of a property. All these definitions go to show us that faith is not something you are hoping for but something that you are holding presently. Whereas hope is future or what you are expecting to have one day, faith says I have it now.

Therefore when you declare that **"by his stripes I am healed"**, or **"I command that money to come to me"** or **"that car is mine"**, it means you are not trying to get it but you already have it.

I bet you that anyone who has this understanding will never say his spoken words never came to pass.

The point is that you are not speaking so that it will manifest, you are already speaking what is real to you although it is yet to become real in the physical realm.

As long as it is real to you by faith, you know for sure that it will definitely manifest in the physical realm. Our Lord Jesus Christ gave us a perfect model of how to mix faith with our words according to Mark 11.

Now the next day, when they had come out from Bethany, He was hungry. 13 And seeing from afar a fig tree having leaves, He went to see if perhaps He would find something on it. When He came to it, He found nothing but leaves, for it was not the season for figs. 14 In response Jesus said to it, let no one eat fruit from you ever again. And His disciples heard it. Mk 11:12–14

In the above scripture we see Jesus speak to a fig tree which refused to bear fruit; in fact he cursed the tree to death.

We also notice that the disciples heard him but nothing really happened to the tree which could have made the disciples to praise him as they usually do when he does unusual and miraculous things.

In the mind of the disciples, the words of Jesus failed to materialize. They concluded that as for today, the master's words did not produce result.

On the other hand Jesus was also thinking differently. As far as he was concerned, the tree was as good as dead. He was convinced with full assurance that the tree had become what he said. He did not need any other evidence to confirm this because by his faith, evidence had already been tendered.

No wonder the matter was put to rest in his mind. It was his disciples who were shocked when they saw that the tree had started to die from the root the next day.

Now in the morning, as they passed by, they saw the fig tree dried up from the roots. 21 And Peter, remembering, said to Him, Rabbi, look! The fig tree which you cursed has withered away.

Mk 11:20–21

They were shocked because their conviction was based on what they saw. The two things to note here are that, it is either your faith is based on what you see or on what you said. Jesus was never shocked or amazed because his conviction and assurance was founded on his words. He knew that what he said was as real as his body. This is exactly how to properly mix faith with your words.

When the disciples asked Him about it, He told them they should operate the same way. In fact, He said that whosoever (in other words, anyone and everyone, including you and me) will speak believing his words will come to pass will have whatever he says:

So Jesus answered and said to them, have faith in God. 23 For assuredly, I say to you, whoever says to this mountain, be removed and be cast into the sea, and does not doubt in his heart, but believes that those things he says will be done, he will have whatever he says.

Mk 11:22–23

Jesus finally taught us a very powerful secret that if we can properly mix our faith with every word we speak as he did, all our words will surely come to pass.

In other words, Jesus is saying don't speak words and doubt in your mind that it will not come to pass.

According to him, the moment you do that, those words lose their power for manifestation. Rather when you speak, believe that those words are real and with time they will manifest for all to see.

When everyone is complaining about recession and how difficult the economy is, speak words of abundance and have faith that abundance will come to you no matter what happens. As you add faith to those words, it will trigger the manifestation of abundance.

The key point is that every word whether spoken by God or a man will never come to pass until it is properly mixed with faith.

Receive What You Speak

It means that when you speak words of faith concerning any situation or whatever you desire, go ahead and *take it*, believing that you have it from the moment you spoke it.

That is what it means to receive. Then start thanking Him for it. If you have called for a new car or house, rather than continuing to pray, beg and plead for God to give it to you, you should receive (take) it by saying, "thank You, Lord, for my new car and my new house. I believe I have received it. It's mine.

I have it now, in Jesus mighty name. Now does that mean your new car, house or healing will instantly show up in your driveway? Not necessarily. But that doesn't matter. What matters is that in the realm of the spirit, you have already taken possession.

From the moment you said it in your words, it was yours and if you keep saying so, and don't waver no matter what happens, you will be driving the car and living in that house.

This is the same way you receive when it comes to healing, health or any other thing. When you declare that, *"by his stripes I was healed"*. You can go ahead and command that sickness out of your body. That healing is real. Go ahead and say *"Thank You, Lord, for my healing. I take it by faith because it is mine. I believe I have it. Thank you that every symptom is gone from my body."*

Although your physical feelings may not come in line right away, don't get discouraged. Just keep seeing yourself well and use the Word of God and your words to receive the healing you've already taken by faith and your healing will surely manifest to the glory of God.

It sounds simple, and it is. But it's not necessarily easy, especially at first, and here's why. To truly believe that what we say is going to happen, we must have confidence in the power of God's Word and our words, not just when we are praying or making faith confessions, but all the time.

In the next chapter, I will show the final reason why so many people miss out on the manifestation of their words.

CHAPTER SIX

TIMING AND MANIFESTATION

If Satan knows that a person lacks complete understanding about timing and manifestation of their words, he will take advantage over them.

I believe this is one of the main reasons so many people give up on their words the moment there is a delay.

I have consistently shown throughout this book that the words we speak in general come to pass with time. What will help you to endure or wait until your words come to pass is to understand the difference between the time you received by faith and the time it will take before the manifestation of the words.

The lack of this understanding is what makes many people eventually give up when their words are not seen to come to pass according to their expectation. That you received your healing by speaking words of faith does not mean every symptom will disappear immediately.

That you confessed and said "I take possession of my car, house or lands does not mean it will show up the next minute. To help you take possession and see the manifestation of your words there are two different timings you need to understand and how to handle these two timings according to the word of God.

The Receiving Time

The first timing to recognize is the moment you received by faith when you spoke those words. As I stated clearly in the previous chapter whatever you say is real. The moment you said that "by his stripes I was healed", that healing has been given to you, it has been accredited to your account.

So Jesus answered and said to them, have faith in God. 23 For assuredly, I say to you, whoever says to this mountain, be removed and be cast into the sea, and does not doubt in his heart, but believes that those things he says will be done, he will have whatever he says.

Mark 11:22–23.

According to Jesus the time you received what you said was the moment you spoke and not one minute, hour or a day after you spoke. That means while you were speaking, at that same time you received whatever you confessed.

However, this timing is different from the second timing. The first time is when you received by faith. It is when you receive and you are so sure you have it even though no other person can see it.

For what you received instantly to manifest, that takes you to the second timing. Yes, you have that car, house or healing by faith but you need another time to cause it to manifest in the physical realm.

Time for Manifestation

The time for manifestation is the period between the first time you received by faith to the time your words finally comes to pass physically. There was a period between the time Jesus cursed the tree and the time the tree started to wither. In his case, it took almost a day for the tree to start withering.

Now in the morning, as they passed by, they saw the fig tree dried up from the roots. 21 And Peter, remembering, said to Him, Rabbi, look! The fig tree which you cursed has withered away.

Mark 11:20–21

The tree was cursed the previous day. Even though Jesus knew that it was already dead, he needed to wait until the next day before his words came to pass physically.

Therefore recognize that no matter what you said, it will take certain period of time for it to come to pass.

For the vision is yet for an appointed time; But at the end it will speak, and it will not lie. Though it tarries, wait for it; because it will surely come, it will not tarry.
Habakkuk 2:2

God is saying that my son everything that you received by faith has a specific time limit for manifestation. He is calling you to wait until the manifestation comes.

As long as you received it, as long as you can see that car, he said wait for it because it will not delay. That period could be a minute, hour, day or days, several months or even many years depending on what you said and how well you applied the solutions given in this book.

The failure to recognize and understand this simple key is why so many people give up on their words when they fail to see their manifestation.

What do you do during this waiting period? It is not the time to sit down and be looking into the skies for what you said to come to pass, rather it is the time for you to work out what you have received by faith by applying all the keys that have been unveiled to you in this book.

The period of waiting therefore is not a period of resting but a period of working the word. If there is a need for you to stand up and act on the word you spoke, go ahead and do it.

A man of God once said God told him several years ago, if you believe you are healed stand up and begin to walk.

He spoke the word when he saw his healing in the finished work of Christ but there was a need for him to begin to act on what he believed and said. To the glory of God, his healing began to manifest when he began to act the word.

Is this not great news that a man who was declared to go home and die by the physicians of his day reversed that death verdict all by the power of spoken words and working the word?

I see you speaking words to things, situations, and circumstances and they are responding to you. I see your words coming to pass as you speak them boldly. Glory!

Masters over hindrances for instant results

There are some people who have become masters over these hindrances and get instant manifestation of their words.

Many beginners give up when they do not get instant manifestation of their words.

It takes time for a beginner to master and be very effective with the truth of the word of God.

The disciples in the beginning struggled to cast out a demon.

After a while, they were raising the dead.

Many people who have given up on the power of words do so because they just began and wanted instant results.

It doesn't happen instantly. There are things to know and understand so that you can fully operate in the power of words at an optimum level.

As you take this book seriously and meditate to get the word in you, you will grow to the place where your words manifest more quickly.

Please get my book "[Speaking Things Into Existence](#)". It will make your words have potency and power.

It will bless you greatly.

My desire is to see your progress and prosperity and freedom from negative people and circumstances. Because of that, please permit me to introduce two courses that I believe passionately will help you.

1. To cure prayerlessness, an inconsistent prayer life and the pain of not enjoying all that God has made available to you,, click [here](#) *to learn more about my* [3 Day Course](#) *on "How to Overcome* prayerlessness" that will solve the problem of prayerlessness in your life.

2. To overcome the pain of not having enough money to live where you want, eat what you want to eat and be a blessing to the multitudes around you, I have created a [7 Day Financial Abundance Course](#) that will deliver financial abundance to you quickly.

Click [here](#) to learn more about that course.

REVIEW

Because your review is important to help others benefit from these books, please leave a good review here

Please check out my other books on the next page

Other books by Francis Jonah

3 Day Fasting Challenge: How to receive manifestation of answers

How to Have Outrageous Financial Abundance In No Time:Biblical Principles For Immediate And Overwhelming Financial Success

5 Bible Promises, Prayers and Decrees That Will Give You The Best Year Ever: A book for Shaping Every Year Successfully plus devotional (Book Of Promises 1)

Influencing The Unseen Realm: How to Influence The Spirit Realm for Victory in The Physical Realm(Spiritual Success Books)

Prayer That Works: Taking Responsibility For Answered Prayer

Healing The Sick In Five Minutes: How Anyone Can Heal Any Sickness

The Financial Miracle Prayer

The Best Secret To Answered Prayer

The Believer's Authority(Authority Of The Believer, Power And Authority Of The Believer)

The Healing Miracle Prayer

I Shall Not Die: Secrets To Long Life And Overcoming The Fear of Death

Three Straightforward Steps To Outrageous Financial Abundance: Personal Finance (Finance Made Easy Book 1)

Prayers For Financial Miracles: And 3 Ways To Receive Answers Quickly

Book: 3 Point Blueprint For Building Strong Faith: Spiritual:Religious:Christian:Motivational

How To Stop Sinning Effortlessly

The Power Of Faith-Filled Words

All Sin Is Paid For: An Eye Opening Book

Be Happy Now:No More Depression

The Ultimate Christian: How To Win In Every Life Situation: A book full of Revelations

Books:How To Be Free From Sicknesses And Diseases(Divine Health): Divine Health Scriptures

Multiply Your Personal Income In Less Than 30 Days

Ultimate Method To Memorize The Bible Quickly: (How To Learn Scripture Memorization)

Overcoming Emotional Abuse

Passing Exams The Easy Way: 90% and above in exams (Learning Simplified)

Books:Goal Setting For Those In A Hurry To Achieve Fast

Do Something Lest You Do Nothing

Financial Freedom:My Personal Blue-Print Made Easy For Men And Women

[Why Men Go To Hell](#)

[Budgeting Tools And How My Budget Makes Me More Money](#)

[How To Raise Capital In 72 Hours: Quickly and Effectively Raise Capital Easily in Unconventional Ways (Finance Made Easy)](#)

[How To Love Unconditionally](#)

[Financial Independence: The Simple Path I Used To Wealth](#)

Finding Happiness: The Story Of John Miller:
A Christian Fiction

Finance Made Easy (2 Book Series)

FREE GIFTS

Just to say Thank You for downloading my book, I'd like to give you these books for free.

Download these 4 powerful books today for free and give yourself a great future

Click Here Download

Your testimonies will abound. Click Here to see my other books. They have produced many testimonies and I want your testimony to be one too.

Printed in Great Britain
by Amazon

42564090R00079